THE AUTUMN OF SAINT FRANCIS OF ASSISI

The Autumn of SAINT FRANCIS of Assisi

Roderic Petrie, O.F.M.

ST. ANTHONY MESSENGER PRESS

Cincinnati, Ohio

Cover and book design by Mary Alfieri
Cover illustration by Chris Sickels

ISBN 0-86716-305-4

Published by St. Anthony Messenger Press
Printed in the U.S.A.

Contents

INTRODUCTION

A NYONE WHO KNOWS ANYTHING about Francis of Assisi is intrigued and wants to know more about that remarkable personality. G. K. Chesterton considered Francis to be, after Christ, the only true Christian. To be a Christian one need not go to Palestine to visit those places where Jesus was born, lived out his life and died, for Christ transcends time and place to be of every time and every place. But to know Francis it is helpful to visit Umbria in Italy, the province where he spent much of his life, and, in particular, Assisi, the town that gave him a focal point in time.

A few years ago, needing some time in prayer after several years of soup kitchen work in Philadelphia, I spent an entire year in a hermitage called the Carceri, on Mount Subasio, above Assisi. It is a place of caves, a place frequented by Saint Francis. The small friary or convent built there has been continuously inhabited by friars since those days. A Franciscan hermitage is not a place for a solitary hermit but for two, perhaps four persons. I was welcomed there as a year-long retreatant and made part of the community.

During that year it became evident to me that the friars who had lived there over the centuries—men like Saint Francis himself and his companions, such as Leo, Bernard of Quintavale, Sylvester, Rufino and others; friars we honor today, such as Saints Bernardine of Siena, John Capistran, James of the Marches and so many other saints, blesseds and holy friars; and also probably many more spiritually pedestrian followers of Francis—that all of these were not so very different from the friars I lived with that year. They were not men of plaster and golden halos. They were people of personality and temperament, composites of background and Christian vision, perhaps very different from the persons presented to us in the lives of saints.

So I have sought to present some of these friars from history as the real people they might well have been, at least as I came to picture them in my own mind during my extended stay in and around Assisi. This is basically a work of fiction, yet most of the incidents and most of the persons are recorded in the works of Celano and Saint Bonaventure. It is not my intention to pass off the following pages as history, but rather to revisit it and enliven it a bit more.

Particularly, I wanted to give a bit different insight into Saint Francis in portraying him as a more approachable, winsome man coming to the close of his life. Although several years are covered by the telling of past events, the actual amount of time out of the life of Francis comes down to a period of four or five days. But these are very crucial days in the life of Francis and of the Franciscan Order, for they are the days when Francis makes the decision to step aside as leader of the Order he founded and to give the responsibility of governing to someone else. The anguish for himself and for his friends was intense.

With this little book, another building block forming the considerable mountain of works on Saint Francis of Assisi, I hope I might add another perspective to the picture of that unique man and perhaps encourage someone to seek to know him as I have been trying to do for close to fifty years.

Part One

CHAPTER
Ꭷ 1 Ꭷ

ALTHOUGH IT WAS LATE SEPTEMBER, the heat showed no signs of leaving the Rieti Valley. The rutted track, long since turned to powder by ox hooves and cart wheels, ran on ahead of us like a brown ribbon on the skirt of the hills. Now and then the going was a bit difficult, because the road, furrowed by previous rains, had not been properly repaired by the local people; but over the years my feet had become hard, like boots, so I did not mind the rough gravel nor the hot dust. My mouth was gritty from the dust stirred by the three walking ahead of me and picked up by the breeze newly sprung up. Walking, hour after hour, one had a chance to think and pray. And remember. It wasn't so many years ago that I would have been on horseback, letting a strong gelding cover the miles while I sat above the dust. That was when I had gold in my pocket, fine clothes on my back and a name that had been respected in Umbria for generations: Scipione. And I? Rufino de Scipione. But the man trudging behind me had changed all that. Because of him I was walking barefoot when I might have ridden. I wore coarse and patched wool instead of brocade. I had no gold in my pocket; no, nor food in my belly. Because of him. And now none knew me by

the proud name of Scipione, but only as Brother
Rufino, follower of Francis of Assisi.

We had been walking since early morning before
the sun had touched the stone walls and tiled roofs at
Terni, where we had stayed the night with some
hospitable monks. Not a forced march at all, because
happening on a particularly lovely view we would, as
by some sense of agreement, pause to enjoy it, let it
run across our hot eyes as cool water does over the
tongue. Or we would pause to say our prayers from
the psalter that Leo carried in the bundle on his back.

The sun had passed its peak; it must be mid-
afternoon. The rising breeze hinted at a change in the
weather. In another hour we would arrive at Sant'
Urbano. And beyond there, another forty-five minutes
at least, up under the large shelf of rock on the
mountain, lay the caves and huts that were our
destination: the hermitage of the Holy Cave, Sacro
Speco.

Francis had been quiet all morning. Not that he
was one to talk much anyway; he had certainly
changed from when I first knew him. In the old days
he would pour out an avalanche of stories, jokes and
gossip that kept us all laughing, our ears buzzing.
Now he measured out his speech sparingly, as a farmer
sows more carefully as he gets to the last handful of
grain in his apron. But his wit was still as sharp, his
eyes would snap and his whole body accentuate what
he said. Ordinarily he would unthinkingly sing a
snatch of song, usually in French, something he had

learned when on one of his business trips to Provence with his father; or maybe he would sigh or groan if lost in some thought of our Lord's Passion. Today, however, none of that. Walking single file as we were, Francis bringing up the rear, leaving the office of choosing the path to John, powerful of body and gentle of disposition, he was able to be free from our scrutiny.

He was definitely preoccupied. He was less exuberant and effusive since his return from the Holy Land a few weeks ago. Possibly the shortcomings of the Crusaders had depressed him, but I thought that unlikely, for he always reminded us that we should not be saddened by anyone's sins but our own. More likely, I thought, that even in that far-off place rumors of dissension at home had reached him and hastened his return. More than one brother had taken it on himself to carry to Francis' ears reports of privileges from Rome, a falling away from poverty, the rise of factions, the aping of monastic practices. Arriving back in Italy, he soon enough found many of the stories to be true. The many problems of the ever-increasing brotherhood were weights, I was sure, that held down the wings of his spirit as we filed along the dry, rutted road.

Only last evening, after our supper with the monks, as we sat and watched the stars appear in the darkening sky, he said: "God promised Abraham that his descendants would be as numerous one day as those stars. But so shall we friars increase, for God has a special care for us."

One of the stars suddenly fell across the sky and died. Francis sighed and, after a moment's silence, he asked: "Did I ever tell you, Rufino, of my dream about a black hen?"

"No, you never did. What was the dream about?" I asked.

"Some years ago, now, it was soon after the Holy Father gave us his blessing, I was concerned about the number of brothers coming to join us. The Commune of Assisi was increasingly more alarmed at the number of brothers looking for work, and begging when there was none. Not every brother joined for the right motive. Some were barely Christian, and I found it impossible to know each one. It was a constant worry, how to oversee this flock God had given me and how to provide for it.

"And then one night I dreamed of a black hen. She was meager in size and surrounded by dozens of little chicks, most of which ran to her looking for food and for protection under her short wings. Some there were who strayed off, oblivious of the danger and disregarding her call. Try as she might she could not provide for nor protect such a brood. When I awoke, God helped me to understand that the small black hen was I, and the chicks were the many friars coming to this way of life. From that moment on I gave the care of the brothers over to Mother Church, knowing that the task was too much for me, but that the Church, with the wisdom of her years and guided by the Holy

Spirit, would provide for the upbringing of my chicks, the brothers. And so I now try to lead the brothers more by example than by legislation or organization."

Somewhere out among the dark trees an owl called, like a soul looking for God. A lonely sound in the stillness.

"But even as the stars up there are becoming more numerous in the sky as we sit here," Francis went on, "the brothers, too, are becoming more. Each one looks to me for decisions, for correction of wrongdoing, for the settling of disputes, so much so that my every moment could be taken, leaving me not a moment for prayer or to preach the gospel.

"Somehow I believe I do not have many years left. I am not yet forty, but I believe I am reaching the end of the path God has shown me. I have yet to give the brothers what I wish with all my heart to leave them: an example. That is the only way I can care for them now, for the task is beyond my size. I dread to think that even one friar might fall away from our brotherhood because of my poor example."

Now and then we paused in our journey to admire a particularly lovely view that John pointed out to us, but these stops were more for Francis' evident difficulty of keeping up with us than for the scenery. At such times Francis would rouse from his thoughts and, spying a tiny forget-me-not or the leap of a lark from the grass nearby, the mountains rolling purple to the western horizon, he would speak to us of God's providence, beauty and wisdom. "Every creature," he used to say, "is a footprint that shows us that God has passed this way."

Although it was so warm under the sun, Francis nonetheless had the hood of his capuche over his head—not to keep the flies off his freshly shaved head, as I was doing, but to guard his eyes from the sun. Since returning from the East he seemed to be having trouble with his vision. His eyes watered a lot in the sunlight, and I think they gave him pain too, although he did not complain of it. One would never know how he felt, well or ill, if one waited for him to speak of it.

Before us lay Sant' Urbano, a handful of houses sprouting like mushrooms from the stony ridge of a hill. Although our destination lay a bit the other side of it, we nonetheless turned off and followed the narrow alley to the center of town to refresh ourselves at the town well. The townspeople, when they realized that it was Francis washing the dust from his face and hands in their piazza, came scurrying from doorways to get a close look at him. Before many minutes all those who were not off with the sheep or in the fields, fifty or sixty of the very young and very old, were crowding around us. Around Francis, rather, for his fame as a man close to God reached even to these isolated towns. Francis couldn't let the opportunity pass to greet the people, so he pulled himself up on the lip of the well so that all could hear him.

"Peace and comfort, good people. Thank you for sharing with us the water God provides for all his creatures. The rain that God showers on your vines and crops will make for a rich reward for your labors. So don't be ungracious and neglect to give thanks to him when harvest time comes. And don't neglect the soil of your soul, either. Work at planting virtues, care for your sick and unfortunate neighbors, welcome strangers who come hungry to your door so that you will have something put aside for eternal life. Woe to those who store up no spiritual provisions for the future, thinking only of their lands and houses, and do no penance. Fast now before the heavenly banquet; give alms to those in need, for what we give away now we will have to our account when we stand before God. And be at peace with one another, for we are liars if we say we love God and hate our brothers and sisters. Finally, pray for me, Brother Francis, and for the other brothers, that we might grow in the love of God."

He hopped down and we departed from the people of Sant' Urbano, a few of them pressing some bread and pieces of cheese upon us as we left and once more started off along the road that would bring us to the steep path winding to the hermitage above us.

As we walked along, suddenly, one of the men from the village, loosening the soil in his grove of olives alongside the path, caught sight of us filing along the path that bordered his field, and threw down his hoe and ran to intercept us.

"Are you that Brother Francis from Assisi," he asked John, who once again was in the lead, "the one everyone talks about?"

13

"No, I'm Brother John. The one you're looking for is back there, the last brother."

"Ah, you're Brother Francis. Listen, try to be as good as people say you are, for many are trusting in you. So you had better be what they expect of you."

I winced and felt ashamed for the poor fellow that he would be so rude. But not Francis! He was all smiles, as though someone had just given him a great compliment. He grabbed that fellow and hugged him as though he were his dearest friend.

"Thank you, thank you, my dear friend. You are my greatest friend for telling me what I need to hear. I wish everyone could set me straight like that and had my welfare at heart as you have. Pray for me, then, that I do as you say." And giving the peasant another hug, he left the fellow, pleased and satisfied, looking after us.

As we climbed the steep ascent through the woods the shade thrown by the rocky crags above us was already deepening. Behind us, the broad valley, the yellow fields of wheat and the pale green olive groves were still washed with light. Now and then the lonely bleat of a sheep or a querulous bark of a peasant's dog rose from the farms sparsely scattered beneath us. On the far side of the valley, beyond Stroncone, stretched the mountains, gilded by the lowering sun. The expanse of the valley spreading out below us toward Terni and to the south toward Rome made it evident why for centuries hermits, and I suppose brigands, too, had hidden themselves away up here where they could observe the distant comings and goings of armies and travelers while being safely removed from them. A building breeze carried the faraway rumble of thunder. As we climbed up through the quiet woods Francis again lost himself in his concerns. That storm was gathering somewhere behind the mountain, threatening the stillness of the forested crags above us. The steep climb up the mountain's flank, along a path that twisted among the oak trees, had us all dripping with perspiration, even though the air was cooler now.

Arriving at the hermitage, we found everything pretty much as we had left it several months before. Other friars came here from time to time to spend days or weeks in prayerful isolation, perhaps others used it as well for shelter, but whatever guest or pilgrim always left it in good condition. Not that there was much to be disturbed: a small stone hut we ourselves had put up at one side of the little chapel that had been there for many years, built by monks, it was said, fleeing from the iconoclasts somewhere in the East. The well, not deep, but sufficient for our needs. The cave where we would take turns living for more seclusion and prayer. A few simple furnishings and utensils, that was all.

Francis continued up to the bluff above, where another small chapel stood near other caves, so Leo went off with him to be closer at hand if needed. Angelo, John and I busied ourselves with sweeping out the chapel and the hut, putting away the few things we had brought, setting aside some of the bread and cheese the villagers of Sant' Urbano had pressed upon us, along with some olives we had brought with us for our evening meal. Having eaten nothing since morning and walking all day with only a few stops for prayers, the provisions would be a welcome treat for my neglected stomach.

"Come up here," Leo called. "We'll have our evening prayer up here." So we scrambled up the uneven steps to the clearing where stood the other tiny chapel and, off to one side, the cave in which Francis delighted to pray. Of all the many caves and crevices I'd known Francis to use over the years I had known him, none was more dear to him than this one, for he believed that it was formed at the moment of Christ's death, when, as the Gospel says, the earth shook and rocks were rent. And this it was, a rip in the mountain's side where the earth had shuddered and received this wound, a narrow fissure where Francis would hide himself while he spent long hours, entire days and nights, in prayer. He was there at the moment.

"He's not well," whispered Leo. "Since his return from the Holy Land he's not as strong as he was, doesn't have the endurance I remember. And he seems worried."

"I've noticed that, too," John agreed. "Did you notice how preoccupied he seemed all day?"

I said nothing of his conversation with me the night before, not wishing to repeat something that was perhaps not meant to be repeated. But just then Francis emerged from the cave, looking quite drawn, and we went into the chapel for our evening prayer.

Leo, the only priest among us, and so, better able to read, would lead us in our prayers. It was now almost dark in the tiny chapel; what light there was came through the narrow slit of a window behind the crude stone altar, reflected from the valley's fields. The murmur of thunder had become more persistent, the air cooler, and as I knelt in the dank darkness a shiver went up my back. Francis, kneeling close to the altar, outlined against the light, looked too frail to contain the great zeal for God's Kingdom that I knew to be a part of him.

Bowing over, his face close to the stones of the floor, Francis began: "We adore you..." and we took up the greeting he had taught us, "most Holy Lord Jesus Christ, here and in all your churches throughout the whole world, and we bless you, for by your holy cross you have redeemed the world." There was no need to light the oil lamp that hung from the ceiling, for we knew by heart the psalms that Leo began. The Latin, not so greatly different from our own way of speaking in the Umbrian Valley, filled the little chapel with its soothing cadence. I could recall the times as a young boy when my family would stay overnight in Assisi at my Uncle Favarone's house on the piazza of San Rufino. At night, just before bed, we could hear the canons in the church singing Compline. Even then, my cousin Clare, only recently returned with her family from exile in Perugia, wanted to stop our whispering and listen to the lilting chant. So we would join, as best we could, in singing the final hymn to Mary. Now, of course, Clare sang Compline every night, but with the Ladies who had joined her in the cloister at San Damiano outside Assisi's walls.

Lightning ripped across the sky and thunder banged against the chapel like a fist. "Into your hands I commend my spirit," we repeated after Leo. Yes, Lord, I have put my life into your hands. When I asked Francis here to be one of his companions, it was because I wanted to give myself fully into your hands. I have learned much from him, from what he says and what he does: in short, I have learned how to be a Christian. If ever he was a fool, a madman, as I have heard people call him, he has grown through that and far beyond that to be "touched" by the madness that comes from You. More and more I have come to see that it is not he who is eccentric, off center, but the rest of us; it is not he who is unbalanced, but the rest of the world that is topsy-turvy.

"You are holy, Lord, the only God," Francis whispered from the base of the altar where he knelt.

"And your deeds are wonderful," we answered.

"You are strong," he sighed.

"You are great," we agreed.

"You are the Most High."

"You are almighty. You, holy Father, are King of Heaven and earth," we added.

"You are three and one, Lord God, all good." Francis now spoke out strongly, speaking to the infinite God in the smallness of the chapel. "You are Good, all Good, supreme Good, Lord God, living and true."

He continued with the praises to God he had composed and we responded to him:

"You are love."

"You are wisdom."

"You are humility."

"You are endurance."

"You are rest, you are peace."

"You are joy and gladness."

"You are justice and moderation."

"You are all our riches, and you suffice for us."

"You are beauty."

"You are gentleness."

"You are our protector."

"You are our guardian and defender."

"You are courage."

"You are our haven and our hope."

"You are our faith, our great consolation."

"You are our eternal life."

"Great and wonderful Lord," he whispered, savoring each word as it passed his lips, "God almighty, merciful Savior."

We knelt there listening to the thunder bounce among the cliffs above us, the death gargle of the dying day. Francis turned to us: "Before departing for this place I sent word for Brother Peter Catanii to join us here. He will probably arrive tomorrow, so watch for him and bring him to me." A bolt of lightning struck outside, burning the air, and a thunder clap made my ears ring.

"Quickly," he urged us, "hurry down to the hut; the rain is beginning. I'll stay here for a while to listen to Brother Wind whistle at the door as Sister Rain dances on the roof."

So off we ran, leaving Francis there alone, diving into the hut as the sky opened and poured down the rain it had withheld for weeks.

CHAPTER
2

THERE IS SOMETHING TO BEING DRY, a fire crackling on the hearth while rain drums furiously on the roof, that is peaceful and comforting. The fire smacked its lips and ran its tongue along a log Angelo had brought to the fireplace. Our shadows leapt and swayed upon the wall. Thanking God for the food we had to eat and praying for those who had given it, we sat cross-legged on the floor, eating and listening to the storm lash around us. My thoughts returned to Francis' last words about the arrival of Brother Peter. Why was he coming here, to this out-of-the-way place to confer with Francis? Did the meeting have anything to do with Francis' evident preoccupation along the road?

I had known Brother Peter since I joined Francis. He, too, was one of the first of the companions. He was a well-educated man, astute and prudent, to whom others turned when Francis was away on one of his journeys. He had not been too well of late, I had heard, but he was by no means an old man yet, and full of energy, like Francis.

In the woods nearby some rocks gave way, loosened by the rain, and went bouncing, crashing down the mountain into the trees. The noise nudged a memory in me and I must have winced, for Leo said:

"Yes, Rufino, we all discovered that day how easily we can be tricked by the devil and how close to God is Francis."

Francis had been busy going about preaching that summer, eight years ago now, in the towns and markets that lie between Assisi and the Arno River. Returning fatigued to St. Mary of the Angels, he had asked Leo and me to accompany him to the caves above Assisi on the slope of Mount Subasio. Brother Masseo, and of course Brothers Bernard and Sylvester, who spent most of their time in seclusion, were already there. It would be good to see them again, to bring them some provisions and the greetings from their families in Assisi. And it would be good for me, too, to get away to the quiet forest where there were no lepers to care for. I needed to think and to pray.

How long had I known Francis back then? I'd known about him, of course, for a long time; that is, I had known who he was. His father owned several properties near my family's holdings, so I sometimes saw him visiting the farms with his father Pietro Bernardone. The older man always dressed rather plainly, although his clothes were of the very best material. Francis, however, without being foppish, liked bright colors and the latest styles. They were merchants, basically, the Bernardones. They owned a lot of land, too, but theirs was not a family of long history like my own. The grandfather had also been a merchant and a craftsman of some sort; a weaver, I think. Not much history behind them, no, not like my own. And after all, that mattered. As my father used to say, after the Bernardones had ridden off on their fine horses: "It isn't how much gold one has but one's family name that is important." The Bernardones, with all their gold and lands, were nobodies.

Later, when I was older and attended some of the holidays and festivals up in Assisi, I got to know Francis better. He was a likable person: full of fun, the instigator of pranks and good times, generous to a fault. Many a time he would pay the bill at a tavern, overlooking the fact that his turn seemed to come around more often than others'. One couldn't help but like him, although I couldn't take seriously his bravado about what he would do to win his spurs if it should come to war again with Perugia. Yes, I got to know him and his family rather well.

That was my problem. I knew Francis. I knew his father, a shrewd and calculating businessman. Wealthy, yes, but still as common as Assisi clay. I knew his mother, a lovely and gracious woman, a good balance to her irascible husband. But she, too, was the daughter of a French merchant from Toulouse. I knew Francis' brothers, made to the image of their father. And Francis, for all his fine clothes and generous party giving, for all his posturing and predictions of a knighthood, for all his undeniable good qualities, was of the same Assisi clay.

We did go off to war against Perugia in November of 1202. The leaders of the Commune believed that Perugia's own internal problems would sufficiently divide, sapping its ability to fight, so that we could regain the lands taken from us a few years previous. So the knights of the Commune and any man from the area who wanted to join us rode off one day with the bishop's blessing to see what havoc we could wage against our long-time enemy. Francis was among us, suited in the best of armor and on a strong horse, looking more knightly than any of us.

Oh, it was a lovely day, I recall. One of those days in Umbria when the sky is bluer than a bluejay's back and the sun sparkles on the autumn's first frost. With our banners and our polished armor we made, I'm sure, a beautiful, a heroic picture as we rode off up the valley. It's at such moments, removed from combat and carnage, that war seems noble and honorable.

As we rounded the bend of the road skirting Collestrada we rode directly into the forces of Perugia. They were waiting for us. Any beauty in the scene, the knights drawn up in battle formation, their banners to the wind and the sunlight reflecting from shields and swords, was lost on me. I was numb from head to heels, terrified by the sudden realization that we were going to do combat; that this was not a holiday tournament but a war and some of us, I, might get killed.

Suddenly, from somewhere behind me, I heard Francis' voice like a trumpet: "For God and for Assisi! Charge!" And with that he spurred his horse through us toward the Perugians and we were all caught up in a wild, undisciplined explosion toward the enemy. I

24

remember getting my sword from its scabbard and singling out a clumsy-looking adversary bestride a work horse, but as I bore down on him the work horse became a battle-trained charger and the figure behind the battered shield took on the dimensions of a giant. In his right hand he held a large broadsword and I recall seeing the flat of it, thank God, coming toward my head. That is all I remember of the battle of Collestrada.

When I came to, my head aching and my ears still ringing, I was lying on my back in the warm sunshine. Francis' concerned face was peering down into my own. "Are you all right?" he asked. "We were harvested like ripe olives." Raising myself on an elbow, I saw seated and lying around us our entire "army." We were prisoners. What a debacle!

One entire year I spent in prison in Perugia before those of us who could negotiate a ransom, Francis among us, were allowed to return to our homes. But it was during that year that I got to know a Francis I'd never known before. It was Francis who did not give in to depression but cheered the rest of us, chafing under the imprisonment, with his songs and jokes. Although he is not noble, I must admit that he acted with more courtesy than many who prided themselves on their family coats of arms. It was Francis, when quarrels would erupt, who was the pacifier and arbiter. When we began to isolate one for his difficult and arrogant ways, it was Francis who befriended him.

Difficult times bring common sufferers closer

together. So it was that when we were released I stayed in touch with Francis and was interested in his welfare during his subsequent illness and the difficulties he started to have with his father. It seemed that Francis could not settle down. Neither his life at home or in the shop, his good times with us on a Saturday night, not even his dreams of being a knight seemed to hold his interest anymore. He seemed indecisive, confused. His boasts of one day becoming a great knight, an important person, became less credible. Even he didn't seem to believe his predictions. Instead of joining in the parties as he once had so happily, he would go off by himself, returning in the evening subdued and incommunicative. He no longer was interested in the family business, sometimes giving the day's profits to any beggar who asked for alms.

"He's ill," claimed his mother. "It's a fever he must have caught in prison. He needs a physic."

"Yes, he's sick," ranted his father, "sick in the head. What he needs is a good beating!"

"Maybe he's in love and he's thinking of getting married."

"Yes," agreed Francis, but without conviction, "perhaps I'm in love and fearful of getting married."

Finally he broke with his father and went to live in the tumbled-down church of San Damiano. But it was not a clean break, for his father accused him of stealing, of running off with the profits from a sale of cloth, and demanded justice. Now spending his time rebuilding the little church, Francis decided that he was not answerable to the city's judge. So off they went to the bishop, and there—I'll remember the scene till I die—in the courtyard of the bishop's house, Francis not only returned to his father the money from the sale but also the clothes on his back as well. And walking away as naked as the day he came into this world, he said: "From now on I'll call no man father, but say only 'Our Father, who art in Heaven.'"

Well, Francis followed his own road for the next two years, rebuilding abandoned churches, begging his food in the streets of Assisi. And I walked my way, shouldering my duties on my family's estate.

Then our paths crossed once again, joined, and we walked the same way, the narrow way of the gospel. I left my family home, my plans, as so many have done, to join Francis, and we formed a brotherhood: the Penitents of Assisi.

It was exciting, a challenge, a novelty, to say the least, to be a pauper for the sake of an ideal, along with friends who knew me. For a time, because it was new, the hard life was easy, even fun. We vied with one another to sleep the least, beg the most, be the poorest. Then the empty stomach, the thin and patched clothing, the lack of a place to call home became our daily experience—no longer exciting, a hardship. It was then that the mouse of doubt started feeding on my entrails. Francis was, after all, a common man; no matter what stories one told about him or how one colored him, he was of common clay. By what right was he a leader? How did he come by any deeper insights than I? What if he is deceiving himself? Or what if, God forbid, the devil is deceiving him? Where would that leave the rest of us? Where would that leave me? I needed to get away, to think and to pray. I needed God to speak to me.

We started off early the next morning, taking the path to the bottom gate into Assisi, past the bishop's residence with its memories and the church of St. Mary Major. Coming to the main piazza, without a glance toward Francis' home, we continued on toward San Rufino. The street was already filling with the stalls of farmers and merchants, with people coming to do their shopping, so we saw many we knew. Some greeted us, others merely watched us pass, noncommittal in their opinion of us. Up through the piazza of San Rufino we went, past my uncle's house, when an upstairs shutter banged open and my cousin Clare put her head out, the sunlight catching in her blond hair. Nearly seventeen, she will soon make some lucky fellow a beautiful bride, I thought, as I waved to her.

"Rufino, cousin Rufino," she called. "Wait, wait just a moment for me. I'm coming down."

I had no wish to go into the house, for too many times had I held fruitless "discussions" with my uncle and cousins, Clare's brothers, about my leaving home to join Francis. These "discussions" (rather than call them arguments, which they truly were) never settled anything. No, far better to stand here in the warm sun, to listen to the noisy starlings busy with their young up in the bell tower, than to chance a heated argument and my uncle's shouts.

The solid door creaked and out bounced Clare, her younger sister Agnes with her. Agnes was the more demure of the two; Clare, like the sunlit morning, was charged with energy and excitement. In her hands she held a wide loaf of bread, its thick crust yellow-brown like ripe wheat.

"I'm so glad I saw you," she beamed. "I baked this loaf just this morning to give to some poor person and who is more poor than you, Rufino? Please take it for yourself and the other brothers."

I was delighted to accept the unlooked-for alms, for we had left with nothing, relying on what God might provide. And here it was. Too, this saved us from begging, something I was still sensitive about doing from people who knew me and my family.

Turning her attention to Francis and Leo, Clare greeted them and said to Francis: "Brother Francis, I want to thank you for stopping here yesterday on your way from Gubbio to preach in the piazza. I listened to you from my window up there." She motioned to the one where she had put out her head.

"Me, too," Agnes assured us, "but I fell asleep."

Francis laughed, saying, "Good morning, Lady Clare. I'm sorry I talked so long, Mistress Agnes. Yes, I saw you both up there, and even now, Lady Clare, I have to look up to see your face." Clare was a good bit taller than Francis and, although not a bit self-conscious, she blushed. Probably, I guessed, because she had a ready retort for Francis' short stature, and hesitated to give back as good as he gave her.

"I'm glad to see," he continued, with a sly look at me, "that you give some of your time to do things for the poor rather than spend it all filling a hope chest."

"I was hoping, Brother Francis," Clare went on as though he had not spoken, "that I might get the opportunity to talk with you. You said yesterday when you were preaching that one is pure of heart if she has no time for the things of this world but is always busy with the things of heaven. It seems to me that those of us who cannot give up our families, our homes, as Rufino has done, are held prisoner by our obligations. My parents suggest one man after another to me, some I know and some I've never met, as a possible husband. I have to consider 'the things of this world,' as you say. How I'd love to go off with you today, up to the mountain, and spend the day thinking of 'the things of heaven.' But I don't have the freedom to do that. I am not a bird, like those in the bell tower up there, free to spend my time chirping and flitting about."

"It's true, Lady Clare, much is expected of you. Those birds up there don't merely fly about enjoying their leisure; they are occupied all day in the labor of feeding themselves and their young, the same as the hard working citizens of Assisi. The difference is that while they gather their food they sing praises to God, and when they feed their young, they sing a hymn of thanksgiving. We, on the other hand, not only do not praise God for what he gives us, but scheme to get our

30

brothers' share as well. Your parents are right. You should have a bridegroom. Perhaps you have overlooked the most noble and richest of them all. Once married to him you would be free of care and able to give your time to the things of heaven. Thank you for the bread. We will repay you with our gratitude and prayers. God's peace, Lady Clare, Mistress Agnes."

"Just a minute, Brother Francis," Clare said, catching him by the sleeve. "Whom are you suggesting? He can't be from Assisi, for father has dragged everyone between sixteen and sixty for miles around to meet me. It's humiliating. I feel like a bolt of cloth in your father's shop. And there's not one I would want to marry."

"Then I will introduce you. He is a very good friend of ours." With that he turned and started up the road beside San Rufino toward the gate that let out on the rough track that wound up through the olive groves and into the forest that covers Mount Subasio.

Catching up to him, I had to appease my curiosity. "Who is this rich nobleman you're thinking of as a husband for my cousin, Francis? If he is such a good friend of ours, I can't think who it could be!"

"Of course you know him, Rufino," Francis laughed. "The perfect bridegroom for Lady Clare would be the Lord."

"God?" I cried. "Are you crazy? My uncle would kill her. He would kill us! Clare can't enter a convent! She's his favorite! Francis, you don't know what you're saying! Who do you think you are?"

"Rufino, I know who I am. I am nothing. But I also know who God is. Lady Clare and God were meant for each other."

Looking back, I could still see Clare looking, not at us, but at the distant heights of Mount Subasio.

The distance to the caves is not great, only about four kilometers, but the morning sun was now quite hot, and long before we reached the shade of the oak forest I was wet with sweat, my heart pounding. The fields of crimson poppies and gray-green olive trees gave way to violets and pink cyclamens under the dark oaks. Now and then I looked back on Assisi and the Umbrian region where plumes of smoke rose here and there into the clear sky. Farmers were burning the stubble from their fields. It was such a transparent day that I could almost count the windows of the houses in Perugia twenty-four kilometers up the valley. And beyond, the mountains tumbled one upon another in a purple heap.

Once into the forest it was cooler. At times the sun seeped through the leaves and splattered on the slight trace of a path that brought us to a small clearing under the face of a cliff. The edge of the clearing fell to a chasm that widened to the valley below. Far out in the valley I could make out my parents' home and I wondered what my mother was preparing for dinner in the roomy kitchen. A trickle of water gurgled across the open space from the cliff and, tucked against the cliff, was a one-room shelter some of us had built last summer. Next to the hut, on the edge of the chasm, stood the tiny chapel that Francis had made, dedicated to our Lady, where Leo or Sylvester celebrated Mass for us. And under the chapel, in the face of the cliff, was a cave, one of several up here, the cave where Francis, when he was first wrestling with what he should do with himself and still regaining his health after that year of imprisonment in Perugia, used to come. There, hidden away for hours at a time, God had his way with Francis, closing some doors to him, opening others.

The only sounds were the occasional chirp of a bird off in the forest across the chasm and the splash of water as it fell upon stones below in the gorge. The quiet was a garment I wanted to pull around me and over my ears.

A call soon brought Masseo, Bernard and Sylvester from their retreats. For the latter two, both from Assisi, we brought news of their families, and to Masseo, who had the task of cook that week, I gave the bread. Then we separated: Francis scrambling down into the cave beneath the chapel, Leo to a cave in the forest across the chasm. I went to a cave farther up the gorge, one near Masseo's, a mere crevice under the overhanging cliff, actually, but adequate for getting out of the rain and for sleeping at night; for during the day I liked to be out in the forest. I wanted to be by myself to think and to pray.

We had been there several days when it happened. I had been avoiding Francis, Leo and the others as much as I could, feeling more and more depressed. What was I accomplishing with my life? Down in the valley was a comfortable home, a mother and father who were getting on in years and who could use my help to manage their properties. And here I was with a name respected in the area for centuries, with an inheritance, following a merchant's son, perhaps deluded, to live like a rabbit among the rocks. If I must leave home wouldn't I do better to be a priest, to provide for others' souls? Or at least a monk with an approved and respected way of life? But I had promised God I would be obedient to Francis, that I would be chaste and utterly free of possessions. Had I done the right thing? And then, as I say, it happened. Jesus appeared to me one day as I was praying in the forest!

"Rufino!" a voice said behind me. It scared me half to death, for I thought I was alone, and, looking around, I saw Jesus standing nearby. I recognized him immediately, for he looked just as in one of the frescoes down at St. Mary Major in Assisi: shining bright, a white cloth wrapped around him and his wounds clearly visible. I was on my knees in the blink of an eye.

"Rufino, you are quite right to be wary of Francis. Fortunately your better breeding and background are coming to your aid. Why are you involved in all this nonsense: dishonoring your duties to your parents, living like a madman—worse, like an animal in a hole in the earth? Look at these wounds, Rufino. Don't you believe my suffering, the price I paid, already sufficient for your sins? Do you have to now debase the human nature I ennobled when I became man? How long will you go on listening to Francis and end up as deranged as he is? I warn you, you will finish where he will: in hell! I forbid you to listen to him anymore, for the sake of your soul!"

Although I knew well enough that I did not deserve any revelations, I confess I felt pleased with myself that God rewarded my many hours of prayer, and rather proud that I had been singled out for a vision, although I was a sinner. But, clearly, I was as good as Francis! Strangely enough, the occurrence brought me no peace. Rather, I was even more disturbed. My fears about following Francis were confirmed: He was not called by God. He was self-deluded, or worse, deluded by the devil. And yet I loved Francis. I knew him as an honest man, a man sincerely trying to serve God and to do his will. Where did he go wrong? Was it simply that as a merchant, a common and poorly educated person, he was beyond his depth? And what of me? What of all of us who had promised him obedience? Hadn't we really promised not Francis, but God, to live this way?

That was on a Monday. Studiously I avoided Francis, letting it be known that I wished to be excused from the communal meetings for the sake of solitude. Jesus came back each day, enforcing the same warning, that Francis was sure to lead me into hell if I listened to him and that I must avoid him. But even the presence of Jesus, which I had prayed to enjoy for so many years, brought me no peace; it brought only the building conviction that sooner or later I must split from the way along which Francis was leading me.

On Thursday, about noon, Francis called up to me. "Rufino, Rufino, please come down to me." Not a move I made. Christ, after all, had warned me to listen no more to him, and although it saddened me to ignore the call, I had to obey the Lord.

"Rufino, Brother Rufino," the voice shortly came again. "I command you under the obedience you promised God to come down to me." Now there was another matter! Obedience. I had promised Francis obedience and, through him, promised it to God; so surely for being obedient to Francis God could not hold me at fault. I did not even know what it was Francis wanted of me, perhaps to do an errand, so there would be no wrong in that. I went down to him.

Francis, when I arrived, was seated on the step of the chapel carving a wooden bowl. "Here," he gestured to the space beside him, "sit here." Although he had a half-smile, a kindly expression, looking up at me he seemed a bit concerned, too, as he moved over to make room for me.

"I've caught sight of you several times in the woods over there during the past few days, Rufino, and I have asked God to be with you in your prayer. All of us know your love for prayer, so we have been glad for you, although we miss your company. Tell me, will you continue to absent yourself? Will you not share with us this evening some of the wisdom you have gained in your prayer, some of the peace you have found?"

"Thank you, Francis," I stammered, "I would not feel comfortable talking about what I have learned; and as for peace, I have too little to share. I had better stay to myself."

"No peace? But God always brings peace, even in the midst of the most dreadful conflict his presence brings peace. When a soul is with God it is like a fish in the depths of the sea. The surface may be ravaged, tossed by storms, but down below the fish is undisturbed. Torments and troubles cannot disturb the peace of a soul immersed in God. Tell me, did you see something? Have you had in your prayer a vision of some sort?"

"I have," I admitted. "I have seen and talked to Jesus. He appeared to me just as he is in that painting above the altar at St. Mary Major, all shining and showing his wounds. But what he told me I dare not say, lest he be angry with me."

Putting his arm around my shoulders, Francis said: "Dearest Rufino, it is only right that you should long to keep to yourself what happens in your prayer. Let me say only this, for I can say it from my own experience. Be very careful. We are fragile men, slow to understand, easily misled. We must mistrust the extraordinary and content ourselves with the humble way, the narrow gate. That is safest. We must always take our stand on the firm rock of our beliefs, the things we know, so that we will not find ourselves in quicksand. Now we know that Jesus is meek, humble and will not deceive us, for he is the way and the truth. But the devil, on the other hand, is the Father of Lies, a deceiver, and his sin was that of pride. Have you had this vision often?"

"Oh yes," I admitted somewhat proudly. "Daily. After Vespers, when the shadows are beginning to deepen in the forest, he comes and talks to me."

"Rufino, you must test this vision to prove who it is you are talking with. Not only for your own good, but for all of us, for you are our brother and what blessing comes to you blesses us all; but what evil afflicts you harms us as well. Now this is what you must do. You must insult him. You must say to him the grossest, most foul thing you can think of."

"But you can't be serious! I can't do that! How could I offend Christ in such a way? I wouldn't want to be discourteous to anyone, no matter who, let alone to my Lord. I could never offend him!"

"That is exactly the point, Rufino. If this person who is appearing to you is our Savior, the meek Lamb who was slain for our sins, he will not be offended. But if it is the Other, his pride will betray him. Now do as I say and don't be afraid. If I am wrong, may any punishment come down on my head."

Back I went to the cave where I was staying. Across the valley the sun was lowering upon the mountains crowded one behind the other. The dark green oaks about me stood strong and firm, clutching the rock of

Mount Subasio. The solid rock, the tenacious trees, gave me comfort.

"Rufino!" Across the narrow chasm from me stood the Lord, bright as the sun over there in the west. But how severe he looked! My knees trembled.

"I warned you, Rufino, not to speak with that charlatan down there, that blind leader of blind men. Now you, too, will surely know what hell is!"

My heart almost jumped from my mouth. My legs buckled with fright and I was on my knees. To this day I don't know how I did it, but I swallowed hard and out of my mouth came one of the most vile insults I have ever heard. Even as the words came out of me, I was ashamed that I could say such a thing and I fully expected to be struck dead on the spot.

But what a reaction! He screamed at me in violent rage, shook his fist and exploded with a blinding force as though lightning struck the spot where he stood. The earth convulsed under me, knocking me flat, and there was such a bang and a roar that my head ached. Down the mountain hurtled loosened rocks and boulders, crashing through the trees, half filling the chasm, to lie piled in a heap below the cave. God of Mercy, it was Satan! It had been the devil appearing to me all those times. And somehow Francis had known!

I scrambled to my feet, but immediately had to sit on a rock. My legs were shaking too much to hold me. All was still.

Covering my face with my hands as a cloud of dust settled around me, I wept in relief and for shame.

"Rufino," a quiet voice said. "Dear Rufino."

Uncovering my face I saw, hovering a bit off the ground, Jesus, fixed to a cross. Far from being afraid, I felt a peace well up in me that is still with me to this day. I brimmed over with a joy I had never before experienced. I knew that this time I was not mistaken, that this truly was Christ.

"Rufino, my dearest brother, Francis prayed for you. He knew that you were being tempted; it is by his prayers you were able to overcome. I promise you, Rufino, that never again will you be so tempted; never again will you be deceived. Do not hesitate to put your trust in Francis. Of all who follow me, he has discovered the surest way." And he disappeared.

Hearing a noise behind me, I turned to see Francis coming down the path to the cave. What a hug I gave him and I told him what had happened, showing him the pile of rocks that had tumbled down the mountain.

"Rufino, come back with me to the hut. We will call Brother Leo to join us; Bernard and Sylvester have come up from their hermitages below. Let's have something to eat to celebrate and maybe Brother Masseo will sing some of his songs for us."

CHAPTER

3

A LOG, BURNT THROUGH, fell to the bottom of the hearth, sending sparks up the chimney. Startled, I came back to myself.

"Yes, Leo, they are very close, God and Francis. It saddens me to see him so tormented. His health is not good, is it? And besides, he seems worried about the brotherhood. What do you think is going to happen?"

"Happen to the brotherhood? I think we must expect many difficulties. We have grown too quickly, we are too many for Francis or anyone to guide effectively. The simple Rule of Life that Pope Innocent approved for us, the discussions at the Chapters we have had, are simply not adequate to govern such a large group as we have become. It is only Francis' personality and example that hold us together, but he can't possibly be present to all the friars in all parts of the world where we've spread. No, he is not well and the task of governing the brotherhood is more than he can manage. I don't know what the answer is, but perhaps Brother Peter will bring that with him when he arrives."

"I think you're right, Leo," agreed Angelo, breaking a stout branch over his knee and tossing the pieces onto the flames. "While Francis was away these past months in the Holy Land, you know yourself how we were like a ship without a rudder, blown here and there. Many of the brothers admire the monks of Saint Benedict or the white monks of Saint Bernard. They think we should be more regulated and disciplined. There are others who don't want to hear the word *rule*; they say the gospel is rule enough. That quarrel and other disagreements are ripping us apart."

"Well I don't care what those brothers say," I retorted. "You know as well as I that Francis won't hear of any of the old rules for us. He says that the way we live was given to him by God himself, and I believe it. If I had wanted to be a monk I would have joined the ones at San Benedetto up on Mount Subasio. Good, holy men they are, but if I am going to live the gospel I want to live it as much like Jesus as I can. I can't do that as a monk confined to a monastery, but with Francis...."

"All right, Rufino," interrupted Angelo, "we have no argument with you. You're perfectly right that God has called us to live in a monastery without walls, to be free to move about among the people as Jesus did. All I'm trying to say is that from the twelve of us who joined with Francis about a dozen years ago at St. Mary of the Angels, we have grown to over twenty thousand spread throughout the world. The simple rule that the pope approved for us back then, good enough for the twelve of us, for we all lived together, no longer suffices to help the new brothers understand and live the gospel as Francis has explained it to us and as we lived it with him."

The rain was lessening, subdued to a steady murmur on the roof. Over by the fire, secure in his own little hermitage, a cricket chirped.

"Then what is going to happen?" I asked.

Leo's silence was no comfort.

The fire purred contentedly among the hard oak logs which at times snapped and popped. Occasionally the shifting wind would throw drops of rain down the chimney, hissing into the flames that danced, yellow, orange and blue, upon the wood. We each became lost in our own thoughts as we sat in the fire's warmth which felt so good. Weather can change in an instant in the Rieti Valley, and this rain had brought the end of the hot spell. Already the air was cooler, fresher.

As in clouds, one can see in flames all sorts of images. Faces appeared, moved, gave way to others. I saw my mother, laughing, lively as a sparrow. My cousin Clare, her blond hair flying. Brother John, John the Simple we called him; one of our earliest companions and already dead. John was positive that the way to be holy was to imitate Francis. When Francis sat, John sat; when Francis coughed, John coughed. Perhaps, in his simple way, John was closer to the essence of living the gospel than any of us.

The hungry flames leapt like racing steeds pulling a fiery chariot.

We had been living, twelve of us, or existing, maybe better said, in an animal shed at Rivo Torto. Returning from Rome after receiving from His

Holiness a blessing on our way of life, we had no place to live. On the road that goes from Foligno to Perugia, just below Assisi and not far from my home, was this tumbled-down shelter for animals which, if it belonged to anyone, none of us could remember. We braced it up as best we could and patched the roof, cleaned it out and made use of it. So small it was that to give a sense of order Francis marked our names on the walls to indicate where each of us slept and prayed.

One evening we were all there but Francis. Bishop Guido had only recently changed the cathedral from St. Mary's to the larger church of San Rufino, and Francis, who was to preach there the next day, had gone to Assisi where he would spend the night praying in a little cell in the cathedral basement. Many of us had already lain down to sleep, for we had worked hard all day helping a farmer nearby repair his roof, and we were tired. Some of us were still awake, praying in our places, before we too retired.

Suddenly through the open door came a burst of fire. I could make out fiery horses and a chariot of fire, and resting in the chariot a burst of light, bright as the sun at noon. Racing at a gallop, the horses and chariot and the globe of light sped two or three times around the tight room. Those of us still awake watched, stupefied, while those who had been sleeping were awakened by the brilliance of the light. And then, exiting through the door, we were left in a darkness made more prominent by the disappearance of the blinding globe in the fiery chariot.

"God protect us," someone whispered. "What was that?"

"Quick, light the lamp," another pleaded.

Bernard discovered sufficient heat in the coals of our outdoor oven to light the wick of our oil lamp and he hung it from a rafter. "What do you suppose that was, and what could it mean?" he asked.

Each of us had his own explanation. It was the prophet Elijah. Or maybe the four horses were those of St. Mark's cathedral and we were being called to Venice. Or certainly the globe of light was the soul of a saint passing to heaven.

But it was Sylvester who convinced us that the vision was of Francis' soul in prayer: luminous and pure, ardent in his love for God and present with us although separated by distance. It was but one more assurance to us that Francis, devoted as he was to God in the way he lived, was even more fervent in his prayer.

John got up to turn out the lamp. It was time for bed.

The next morning the sun was nowhere to be seen. Clouds hung down into the valley like shreds of tattered gray rags, caught in the trees. And above them, more clouds. We were in a limbo, suspended between earth and heaven. All was quiet. I shivered in the chilly air as I pulled up a bucket of water from the well, poured some into a stone basin and began to wash the sleep from me. Leo had gone off to see Francis, John was breaking up some wood and Angelo was trying to rouse some warm ashes back to life. Except for John's efforts there wasn't a sound.

Leo, frowning, came down the crude steps from the upper chapel. "I don't think he slept all night. He's still in the chapel up there where we left him. He must have spent the night praying again. And he looks terrible! He's a sick man, Rufino, or I'm a Barbary ape."

"Well," I said, "I think you're right both times." Leo was short and had more hair on his body than most of us. I hated to let a chance like that slip by me.

Leo dunked my face in the water as I laughed, ending up choking. "There," he said, feeling justified, "that's your penance. But really, Rufino, I don't know what to do. You know he has told me never to disturb him when he's praying, but that doesn't apply to you. Why don't you go up and see if there is something we can do, if we should go ahead with our prayers and Mass without him."

"All right, I'll go, Leo, but I think your father gave you the wrong name. He should have called you Little Lamb." Dodging the kick Leo aimed at me, I went off wiping my face and hands on the hem of my habit.

Just as Leo said, Francis was still in the chapel, sitting on his heels on the flagstone floor. He certainly did look sick, pale, and his cheeks were wet with moisture from his eyes.

"Excuse me, Francis," I said, knocking on the door frame. "Are you all right? Is there something we can do? Will you be joining us for prayer and Mass?"

"Good morning, Rufino," he replied. "I'm all right, thank you. Did Leo send you up here to discover how I am? Well, the truth is that I feel old today, old and worn out and sick. My eyes burned the whole night through, my stomach burned for lack of food and yet my spirit was able to burn with its own fire, God's glory. It is a fire that consumes me, as a flame consumes a candle. So it must be. Do you know what the feast is today?"

"The Transfiguration."

"Yes. During the night I was thinking of this feast, how the Lord showed himself to Peter, James and John in a glorious way, showing them that they, too, would be transfigured if they kept faith in him.

"But God calls us to be transfigured in another way, too. Now, during our lifetime. That is what makes my eye problems, my stomach pains, my fears and worries easier to bear, for they are part of the process of my transfiguration. My soul is the wheat and these trials are the millstones that grind me to a fine flour, transfiguring me into the man God calls me to be.

"And I was thinking of our Sister Clare, too, your cousin. Now there is a transfiguration! Did I ever tell you how she decided to become a nun?"

"No, Francis, you never did. I've always wondered about her change, but I know God can do wonders. Look at what he did in my own life!"

"You remember that day she called to you and gave you a loaf of bread when we were on our way to the caves on Mount Subasio? How I chided her about having the perfect husband for her, and she didn't guess I was talking about God? Well, she would listen to me preach when I would be at San Rufino. Or if she happened to be out shopping she would pause and listen. Now and then she would come up afterward to say hello. We had an ongoing joke about the nobleman I would introduce her to. The better part of a year went by and we came to the season of Lent. The people were preparing for Carnevale. Your aunt, Lady Clare's mother, was redoubling her efforts to point out this fellow and that one as possible husbands.

"I confess that I was having a difficult time to keep my own feet from dancing as I passed one group of revelers after another on my way to San Rufino that evening. In San Rufino Square, outside your uncle's house, were Lady Clare, her family, the whole neighborhood. I must say she was lovely. I greeted them all before going into church where I was going to spend the night in prayer, and Clare asked me with a twinkle—but half in earnest, too, I think—if that rich nobleman was in town for the celebration, and if so, when she would meet him.

"'Lady Clare,' I replied, 'I'll tell you what we'll do. I'll arrange for the two of you to meet tomorrow. He has been anxious to meet you, too. Tomorrow morning, after the bishop gives out the ashes, go to the chapel of the Pietà and wait. You'll meet him there.'

"I saw her brighten immediately and knew she couldn't wait to tell her mother, so that for the rest of the evening she would be free to enjoy herself without any nudgings or whispers to stand straight or smile. I admit I was eager to be on my way, too, for that lady, your aunt, hasn't looked on me with favor since that day I sent you to walk through town in your underpants. Do you remember?"

"Why no, I can't recall walking through the square on market day in nothing but my underwear," I said with some sarcasm. "But what happened with Clare?"

"Well, as I said, I spent the night in the cathedral in prayer. I was saddened somewhat by the thought of what so many were doing that night, that they were missing the importance of being a human being made in God's image. Instead of having merely a good time, some innocent fun before beginning Lent, for many it was an occasion of self-debasement, a transfiguration into something beastly, something less, rather than reaching out to become more. So I prayed for the citizens of Assisi, and for myself.

"The next morning I joined those getting the blessed ashes from the bishop and Clare was among them. There was a freshness to her, like a pink rosebud in the morning. She looked lovely. It struck me that she was a woman now, a very beautiful woman. She would be a lovely bride.

"'Lady Clare,' I said to her, 'if you will wait in the chapel of the Pietà over there, my friend will come and introduce himself. I will join you there in an hour.'

"Off she went and I went to the Blessed Sacrament chapel to pray. Oh, Rufino, how I prayed! I begged God to speak to her heart, to open her heart to his love.

You see, I was convinced that she was really waiting, not for a prince or a rich landowner, but for the Lord of Lords. She just had never met him.

"After an hour I went to the chapel, not knowing what sort of welcome I would receive. When I entered, Lady Clare was on her knees before the statue of the dead Christ laid across the knees of his holy mother. Clare was as still as the statue, as though listening to a voice beyond my hearing.

"'Lady Clare,' I whispered.

"Looking around at me, I saw that she had been weeping. But even so, she smiled at me and, rising to her feet, she said, 'Brother Francis, I truly do not know how to explain this nor how to save you from embarrassment, but I do not care to meet your friend. I've discovered during the past hour that what I truly want to do, have to do, is to belong wholly to God. Like Rufino. It had been a thought that has been stealing into my mind when I left the door unguarded. You think you know us women, Francis, what is good for us and how we should live. But you know next to nothing. Please give my greetings to your friend, and also my apologies. Tell him he is too late.'

"'Well, yes, I see, Lady Clare,' I said. 'You're right, I suppose; I know very little. I'd best go and tell my friend. He'll be disappointed, I know.'

"As soon as the door closed behind me I laughed and danced all the way back to the Blessed Sacrament chapel. I know there was no need to tell the news, but I did want to thank the Lord for his quick action and congratulate him on his new bride. Yes, they were made for each other! And to this day Lady Clare thinks that she escaped by moments from being the wife of a powerful and wealthy prince, from spending her days baking bread and raising children. Sometimes, to tease her, I tell her that my friend did take a bride, a beautiful lady, and they have dozens of lovely daughters. Never has she guessed that she is that bride and the daughters are the other ladies who have come to join her at San Damiano.

"We had better go down to join the others before they send someone else after me," Francis sighed. So we went out into the cool morning silence. "When I think of how the good God has blessed your cousin, Rufino, giving her companions, I marvel. She, perhaps better than any of my friars, has made a friend of Lady Poverty, our Lord's constant companion on earth. She is a remarkable woman, strong, and I must admit that I add to her burden by depriving her of my visits. But that is for her good so that she turns only to God for support and consolation, and not to me. So when you think I am too gruff in my ways with Lady Clare, not doing my duty to those who entered San Damiano, remember that it is for their growth in holiness that they see little of me. As I did for Lady Clare so many years ago, I still pray for her."

"Tell me, Francis," I said, "how are you feeling now? You haven't looked well since your return from the Holy Land."

"The simple truth is, Rufino, that I am not feeling

well at all. My adversary, Brother Body, gets even with me at times for the harsh treatment he has received in the past. Beast of burden that it is, it is lazy, and it is also beginning to show its age. But I'll not coddle it, for it is wily and will try to be my master."

"Yes, you have been severe, Francis, doing far more than you would permit us with your fasts and vigils. Small wonder your body is giving out. You were a far better singer than a warrior," I reminded him.

"Not all wars are won by force of muscle, Rufino. Determination is important, too. But you're right, at heart I'm a singer, a troubadour. I'll have to sing for you and the others a song I have composed in my head," he smiled. "It's about our brother and sister creatures; and better, I think, than any I composed when we were young. Hurry up, let's join the others in prayer. Perhaps Brother Peter has already arrived."

But Brother Peter had not arrived. We had our morning prayer and Leo said Mass for us in the little chapel of St. Catherine next to our hut. How I loved that little church, so small and crude. I had seen the abbey church in Perugia and even been to St. John Lateran in Rome, where one is awed by the immensity of it as one is overcome by God. But this little church was like a worn and comfortable cloak that warmed my spirit. It was built, they say, by monks who fled from the iconoclast heretics of the East, bringing their holy pictures with them and living on this mountain. It was evident that the builders were not skilled masons. They had needed a church, a place to worship and so, using whatever they found at hand, they had put up a church: poor, like themselves; unpretentious, like themselves. But solid and lasting, too, like themselves. Here I felt close to those monks, close to them in the faith for which they must have suffered much and close to the God of us all.

Part Two

CHAPTER
~4~

COMING FROM THE CHAPEL, I saw that the sky was still overcast, while the valley below and the sky above were hidden from sight. A puff of smoke plumed from the chimney of our hut, where John was rousing some coals to life, to merge with the mist overhead. As I went to put out some cheese for our breakfast and the bread left over from last night, there was a shout from the woods. Out of the trees came two friars.

One I recognized at once. He was Peter Catanii. There was a good bit of gray in his red beard and in what little hair he had above his corona. He looked considerably older than Francis, but wiry and hard as a chestnut. His companion was quite young and, from the looks of him, not well enough to keep up with Brother Peter on a mountain path.

"The Lord give you peace, brothers," I said. "You're just in time for breakfast. Come and eat with us."

Francis, coming from the chapel and seeing Peter, ran to him and hugged him. "Peter, thank you for coming to visit me. How was your journey?"

"I thought we would be washed away in that storm last night. A farmer down below was kind

enough to take us in or we might have been out in the
rain all night. But I'm forgetting my manners. I ran
into this young friar a week or two ago. He's
Portuguese, from Lisbon. He was so impressed by the
death of those friars you sent to convert the Moors that
he became one of our fraternity. He even tried to go to
be martyred himself, but God willed it otherwise. He
became ill there in Morocco and, returning to Portugal,
his ship was caught in a storm and washed up in Sicily.
So when you sent word to meet you here I asked him
to accompany me so that he could see the Rieti Valley
where those martyrs came from, and maybe meet their
families. His name is Anthony. A bright fellow, but he
doesn't talk much."

"Peace and well-being to you, Brother Anthony,"
smiled Francis.

Brother Anthony, still gasping for breath, could
only smile a little wanly and bow his head.

"He doesn't look so good, does he?" observed
Peter. "Young fellows today don't seem to have the
energy we used to have. Have you noticed that? But
then he's more of a scholar, I guess, and not used to
running up and down mountains like I am. Say,
Brother Anthony, why don't we have something to eat
with these brothers and rest a little. You look like you
could use both."

Francis, I could see, was enjoying the simplicity
and energy of Brother Peter. Simple he was, a true
Israelite, but intelligent, too. Peter had been one of
those Francis had chosen to direct the brotherhood

while he was away in the Holy Land. That Peter had had problems was inevitable, for he had no real authority. Everyone looked to Francis; when he was absent no one looked elsewhere.

We gathered on the floor before the crackling fire that dispelled the gloom of hanging clouds outside. Brother Peter soon had all of us laughing with his story of where they had stayed last night.

"Delightful family," he was saying. "So poor, yet so happy. Filled with faith, they are. The wife, Concetta, turned out to be a cousin of Brother Berard, who gave his life there in Morocco. Fine lad, wasn't he, Francis? All of them were. I guess the whole valley down there is related to one another. Why, Brother Anthony here couldn't ask enough questions about Brother Berard, what he was like and all. He saw his body, you know, saw those of all the other friars, and helped bury them. Their martyrdom is what gave Anthony here the idea of being one of us. Isn't that right, Brother Anthony?"

Brother Anthony blushed, smiled a little and nodded.

"He doesn't talk much," continued Peter without a pause. "Only when he wants to learn something. Good way to be, I suppose. Not feeling good from that shipwreck of his, either, and of course he doesn't speak our language well. Knows his Latin, though. Yes, sir! Say something in Latin, Anthony."

Anthony, his mouth full of bread, blushed again.

"Well, he had plenty to say this morning," said Peter. "We were sleeping under our host's table when early on their dog chased a cat right across his face. He sat up so quickly that he smacked his head on the table, almost knocked himself silly right there. Well, a jar of oil went flying into the hearth and poof—a ball of fire went up the chimney, scaring the wits out of the wife just going out to milk the cow. She screamed, the dog barked, the cat leapt on her shoulders and we all jumped, thinking the house was on fire. Well, Anthony here had some explaining to do, as best he could, and we all had a good laugh. But you can see the lump on his head there, probably doesn't make him feel good. Might have knocked all his learning right out of his ears for all I know. He's a Doctor of Theology, you know. Very bright. At least he was. He's not used to sleeping under tables in a farmer's kitchen, though, you can tell that."

"I can see that he needs some rest," agreed Francis. "Leo, take our Brother Anthony to the cave beyond the well where he can rest up for the time we'll be here. Brother John, you keep an eye on him and treat him as you would me, to bring him back to health. I think, Brother Peter, I have just the place for Brother Anthony, at Montepaolo up in the Appenine Mountains where the air is clear and cool; there he can teach theology to our young friars while he's regaining his health. When we leave here I'll give him a letter to take along with him.

"As you know, Peter, I have been reluctant to give the friars my permission to study. Not just because some of those who study get puffed up in their heads and begin to think they are better than the brothers who can't read or write, but also because study requires books and books are expensive. Then you have to have a place to keep the books, and before long we would have big monasteries like the Benedictines. That is not our calling. We should have no place of our own, just as Jesus had to live with Saint Peter and had no place to lay his head.

"But if we are going to preach to the people we have to preach the truth, not error, preach what the Scriptures and the Church Councils teach us. So it will be helpful if Brother Anthony will teach the young friars, all in the spirit of holy poverty.

"Now, Peter, let's go talk, you and I. We can go up to the cave God formed for us when the Spirit left our Lord's body. There we can listen to that same Spirit and ask his guidance."

Looking at me and Angelo, Francis said: "Brother Rufino, you and Angelo go down to Sant' Urbano to beg some food so that we can celebrate the arrival of Brother Peter and Brother Anthony. And see if you can borrow a violin," he said over his shoulder as he went off with Brother Peter, "and I'll teach you that song tonight after Vespers."

This wasn't my favorite job, but an order was an order. I knew that begging was good for me; it not only was a way to curb my pride, it also introduced me to some fine and glorious souls.

"Come on, Angelo," I said, "Leo and John will do the work here. Let's get started so we can be back from town before noon."

The tall grass in the path down the mountain was still wet from last night's rain, so before long our habits were wet to our knees, our bare feet coated with mud and bits of grass. Where only yesterday there were none, flowers bloomed and honeybees busily carried off their harvest. We entered into the cloud covering the valley, two shadows gently descending through a silent world until we came out of the mist and onto the road that led back to Sant' Urbano.

Only an hour later we were on our way back to the hermitage. "These people must be some of the finest in Italy," said Angelo. He was elated by the large rabbit he carried in a sack and by a fresh loaf under his arm. Around his neck he had a necklace of onions and peppers. I didn't want to say that the gifts might have more to do with his handsome face and quick smile than with those housewives' Christian generosity, but that was probably the case. I hadn't been so fortunate: half a sausage, a few duck eggs and two eggplants. But the people who gave me this shared with me what little they had for themselves and asked that Brother Francis pray for them.

"Hey, what about the violin?" Angelo demanded, turning around in front of me and stopping. "You said you would ask for one."

"Angelo, I just couldn't ask. I was too ashamed. You know those people saw Francis yesterday, how sickly he looked. And that man warned him to live up to his reputation. They all know that we went up the mountain for silence and prayer. How would it look to take a violin to a sick man going off for some solitude and prayer? They would think I was crazy or that we're up there for a good time. I'll have to tell Francis that I couldn't do it."

"All right, Rufino," Angelo sighed, turning and starting off again. "But you know Francis wouldn't have asked for one on a whim. He must have wanted to hear a violin very badly right now. He's going to be disappointed."

That dark thought, of maybe missing an opportunity to lighten Francis' spirits, made the mist seem darker as we started up the trail once more toward the caves. Well, done is done, I thought. It's too late now. And anyhow, I think I was right. The townspeople would not understand what we, always preaching penance, would want with a violin!

We came out of the mist and the woods into the clearing around our hut. The sun was trying to peek through the clouds overhead. There was some hope for clearing, for there was more light up here and a small breeze was chasing wisps of cloud to a higher altitude.

"Salve," I called, and ducked my head to enter the hut where I could hear Leo and John talking.

"Woof," said something hitting me in the chest and knocking me flat on my back. A huge dog, a wolf maybe, was on top of me trying for a firm grip on the sausage.

"Help!" I hollered. "It's a wolf, he's after our dinner!"

"Bandit, get off him, he's one of us," scolded Leo. "Let go of that sausage and behave yourself. You're going to have to learn new ways."

"Bandit?" I asked, scrambling to my feet and dusting myself off. Thank God the duck eggs were unbroken. The sausage had a few teeth marks in it but seemed otherwise intact.

"Yes, he came while you were away. He seems to have adopted us. I call him Bandit because I think that's how he's accustomed to living, stealing food from the farmers around here. I told him that he is going to have to change his ways if he stays with us. If he does, I'll change his name to something more in keeping with his new personality."

"He'll make a good watchdog," added John.

"Watchdog," I muttered doubtfully. "What do we have that needs watching? And look at the size of him! If he wants to eat regularly he's going to have to go back to his sinful ways. Well, Bandit," I said, delivering up my goods to Leo, who seemed to be doing the cooking, "as far as I'm concerned you're welcome to share what the Lord sends us. Just don't get us in trouble by bringing some neighbor's chicken to our door. And get away from that sack!"

Turning to Leo, I wondered aloud. "You weren't thinking of Lupo, were you, that cutthroat who used to be the terror of the region around our friary at Montecasale, when you named him Bandit?"

"Well," admitted Leo, "I confess that there's something about Bandit that reminded me of Lupo.

Maybe it's the eyes, the way he has of looking you right in the eye like a saint and then stealing the sandals off your feet when you blink. But Francis converted Lupo and the whole band of them, you recall, by being kind to them and sending food to them. When Lupo became one of us everyone took to calling him Brother John because he loved the Lord so much, like the disciple. That's what I'll call Bandit, I'll call him John when he changes his ways."

"Bandit," I said, "I think you've got a ways to go yet." Bandit was showing too much interest in Angelo's rabbit.

"What a beautiful rabbit," Leo said with admiration. "Angelo, that's just the thing. What a meal we'll have for Brother Peter and Brother Anthony. Where's the violin, Rufino?"

"Leo," I said, "forget about the violin. I'll explain to Francis when he comes. Is he still talking with Brother Peter?"

"Yes, they've been at it all morning. It must be something very important if Francis would send for him to come here and spend all this time with him."

Angelo and I went off to the well to clean up while Leo dressed the rabbit for roasting and got the meal together. It wasn't long before the aroma of his efforts drifted from the hut to the well, setting my stomach growling.

John came out to pull the rope attached to the small bell on the chapel roof. Although it had a tiny crack in it, it still made enough noise to call us to our prayers. Leo escorted Bandit out of the hut, leaving him to guard the closed door rather than the rabbit, and joined us in chapel for the Angelus and midday prayer.

We had long ago learned not to wait for Francis past the time of prayers or meals. Sometimes he was so absorbed in his own prayer that the bell went unheard, or he would be ministering to someone wounded on life's highway whom he could not leave unattended. We had scarcely begun when I heard Francis and Brother Peter come into the chapel behind us. Francis' voice seemed stronger, yet Brother Peter's was subdued, as though his mind were elsewhere.

When we came out of the chapel the sun had broken through the clouds. Below us the farms still lay hidden under the mist, but above us the sky was as bright as a bluejay's wing. Bandit bounced over to lick Francis' hand as though they were old friends, and to claim Leo's praise for guarding the door.

As we seated ourselves in a circle on the floor, Leo set before us his efforts.

"Let us give thanks," suggested Francis. "Father of Jesus and our Father, we thank you for this food which our friends in the valley have shared with us. Bless them for their generosity and help them in their needs. And bless us, Lord, in our coming together. May your name be on our lips, your peace in our hearts, your gospel be our comfort and strength. We pray through Christ our Lord."

"Amen," we agreed.

We passed around the olives and bread, first to Brothers Peter and Anthony, our guests. "Do you know," confided Francis, "I think that I would profit from a little wine. And it would suit some news that I have to tell you. Angelo, will you pour us each a little?"

I could see Angelo's ears redden a bit. "Oh, Father, we don't have a drop of wine," he said. "The people around here had such a poor harvest last season that I didn't have the heart to beg any and no one offered me even a cork to smell."

"Very well, Angelo, no matter. We'll enjoy whatever the Lord prepares. Fill our pitcher at the well, then, and we'll quench our thirst with God's water."

So Angelo took the pitcher and hurried off to the well.

"You hardly ever drink wine. This must truly be a special occasion," observed John.

"Well, as you know my eyes no longer see well and my stomach has been complaining. Brother Elias has told me that I must be more thoughtful of Brother Body, for it has served me quite faithfully even though I have been severe with it. Perhaps a bit of wine today would have made amends for the ill treatment.

"Tomorrow we must set out for Assisi where the friars are gathering for our Chapter, so I wanted to be ready for the trip. There I will tell all the assembled friars the news I want to share with you today. But if there's no wine, well, we are fortunate to have Sister

Water join us instead. Ah, here's Angelo."

We all held out our bowls for some water. Francis, being closest to the door, made the sign of the cross over the pitcher, saying, "May God bless you, Sister Water, so chaste and pure, and we thank you for taking away our thirst." Angelo poured into his cup and all of us could see as Francis held it up in the sunshine from the open door that what gushed out was as red as a ruby. It was not water, it was wine!

Angelo stood as though frozen. We all were completely motionless, breathless, for the length of a Glory Be. Then a peaceful smile came to Francis' face and as he lowered the cup to his lap I saw a tear slip down his cheek and into his beard.

"Give to the others," he said.

Angelo, dazed, came around to the rest of us, alternately smelling the pitcher and looking into it until he came to his own place and sat down.

Francis took a sip from his bowl and we followed suit. Looking around at us, he said, so softly I could barely hear him, "Brothers, we mustn't be distracted by this wine that God has given us, nor that Sister Water gave herself over to God so willingly for his purposes. Moses was not hindered by a bush all afire yet unconsumed; rather, he gave his attention to the One speaking from the bush who named himself 'I Am.' These creatures of water and wine, of bush and fire, are the doors God gives us to come to him, the final Reality. How sad those who never pass beyond them, past the immediate realities of a hunger in their stomachs or the feel of silk on their backs; never pass beyond ambitions for their children or hatred for their enemies. They hear the song of the lark and admire the color of the rose, but they do not acknowledge the One to whom the lark sings and for whom the rose blooms. Reality for them is merely that which they see and smell and touch, but such things are shadows of the great Reality. We fall into the same pit when we concern ourselves with what so many consider to be important: increasing our numbers, being scholars instead of unlettered, having influential friends and so on. The reality of ourselves is that we are a worthless lot made precious only by the choice of God who sent his Son to be one of us."

It seemed that even the fire had ceased to crackle, that the room and all of us in it held our breaths to hear what Francis was bringing up from his heart.

"You know that God forbade the Israelites to make any images of him. Why do you think that was? Not just because they might one day worship the statue instead of him, but because a statue would limit him in their minds. They would confine him to be what they could fashion with their hands, a creation of his creatures. He would lose his freedom to be God. We have to allow God to be free to be himself, just as he gives us the freedom to be what we wish: perfectly human, that is, a saint, or to be a caricature of a human, a sinner. When we love someone, truly love someone, we give that person freedom, as the Prodigal's father did. When we try to possess another, that is not love but enslavement; we try to limit the other's potential to become more alive, more free to respond to God's call to holiness. We fear that if the other is free we will lose something of ourselves, for we are seeing the other only as a creature and not as a door that leads to God."

Peter, a bright man, was nodding his head in agreement, like a schoolboy learning his lessons.

"Just as Brother Sun exposes to us the realities of our world, and without his light in the darkness we stumble about, it is our Brother Jesus, the Light of the world, who shows to us the realities of life. Realities can be harsh and cruel, as death and injury; as well as beautiful and gentle, as a violet or a May breeze. Realities must be accepted, brothers. We cannot flee from what is real and hide in what is false, untrue. Yes, in reality lies God, who is truth. In untruth, in deception, is the Father of Lies. If we deceive ourselves, if we ourselves are untrue, how can God be in us? It is in the way life is, in the way we are, that we find God and God finds us. The way of pretense, the denial of truth, leads to self-deception and away from God."

Bandit thumped his tail on the floor as if to say that he agreed and that from now on we would see a different Bandit.

"Of all people," Francis continued, "we who have rejected the falsity of this world and spend so much time aside from its flow, we must be the greatest realists. If we are not firmly grounded in the supreme

Reality by whom we interpret everything around us, we bear more danger than anyone of spinning off into error.

"That is one more reason why I insist that we honor Lady Poverty. It is she who opens our eyes to the truth and value of life. When we are no longer poor we will have fallen into the trap of accepting the husk for the kernel of life.

"The poor man knows better than the rich man what is truly worthwhile. The rich man wants a ring for his finger; the poor man wants work for his hands. The rich man delights in being known for how much gold he has and the grandeur of his house; the poor man takes pleasure in being upright and just."

How glad I was that Brother Anthony was with us to hear Francis speaking from his heart. Up to now he had only heard others talk about Francis' deep insights. He was absorbing every word.

"Aren't we wiser to be poor? Aren't we then better able to concern ourselves with the world as it truly is, with peoples' true needs, when we strip ourselves down to our unadorned selves? Aren't we wiser to be simple? When one dresses his hair and bedecks his body with fine clothing, this sack of bones that will soon die and rot, whom do we deceive but ourselves?

"The reality of the matter is that I am different from Brother Bandit there because of the soul God has given me. When Brother Bandit and I die, my flesh will decay and feed worms just as his. But my spirit will be freed to live forever while his will cease to be.

"So isn't it foolish to give special attention to the flesh and neglect the spirit? We are wise enough to savor the meat of the chestnut and throw the shell into the fire, but when we deal with ourselves, we are apt to cherish the body and give our souls over to be burned."

He paused and blinked his eyes, looking around at us, as though his eyes had been focused on some place far beyond the little room.

"I'm sorry. The wine must have made my tongue too limber. But the Lord is so attentive, is he not? Like a mother is he to us. Angelo, Leo, John, Rufino, I want to tell you why Brother Peter has visited us here. And this will touch on you, too, Brother Anthony.

"When I set out for the Holy Land I did not know exactly where it was. How could I know? I had never been there. All I knew was that it lay to the east, a long way across the sea. But I set out with confidence, putting my trust in others who had been there and in the friars who traveled with me, that together we would overcome any difficulty and arrive at our destination. And so it was. Following the route others had used, avoiding dangers others had suffered, we were safe.

"Our brotherhood is increasing rapidly. Just a few years ago we were but a handful, but now there are thousands. I am like a small hen under whose wings too many chicks seek protection. The task of governing the brotherhood is beyond me.

"Too, although you have been good enough not to

mention it, you cannot have failed to notice that I am not as strong as I was. My eyes do not serve me as they once did, and Brother Body seems less able to obey me. It is no longer a matter of fatigue or laziness, but a growing companionship with Sister Death.

"The government of the brotherhood is more than I can manage. But what I can do is indicate the way to go. God has shown me the way to live the gospel. The other brothers, those I do not know, those who are yet to join us, need the way marked out so that they can make their pilgrimage to God along the route I have taken, pointing out the dangers. I believe God will strengthen me to give the example the brothers need, for it is in example that I can serve them better than by governing.

"Nonetheless, the brothers need someone to serve them in other ways: to listen to them and decide how we can serve the Church. Brother Peter here has agreed, under obedience, I have to admit, to take that burden from me. Believe me, I do not come to this decision because I do not care for the brothers or our Order; it is precisely because I do love you and am anxious to secure the Order's future that I want to step aside. One day Sister Death will take me to the side of Christ, or perhaps I will become so sick that I can no longer work. Far better that the change happen now while I am still able to give example and advice on how to live our way of the gospel."

Anthony seemed to be having some trouble following Francis. I guess his life was taking so many twists and turns that he was fairly dizzy by this time. Being in the presence of Francis, seeing a miracle happen before his eyes and now hearing Francis planning to step aside as leader of the brothers became too much for him.

"Father Francis," he said, "please excuse me. I am not used to the language of Umbria, so perhaps I did not understand. Are you saying that you will no longer be one of us, not a Little Brother? What will you do? What will become of us?"

"No, no, Brother Anthony," Francis quickly assured him. "Our merciful Lord has called me to live the gospel with brothers, with you. God forbid that I take my hand from the plow! But I am saying I must give the government of the brothers over to another, for it is a work too great for my strength. Without those obligations I will be able to be even more of a brother to you and the others."

We all sat there still in our places as the silence rose above our ears. I felt an ache in the area of my heart, the weight of sadness, and I knew tears were ready to spill out of my eyes if I didn't do something.

"Well," I said, "let's toast our brother Peter here. This wine the Lord has provided should gladden our hearts. Brother Peter, I know that you would accept this work only out of obedience and love for Francis. May God, who is so solicitous, support you with wisdom and courage."

"Amen!" everyone said.

"And Francis," I said, "you are not only our

brother, in a special way you are our father. Some will be happy to see you step aside. But we need to be corrected, even chastised sometimes. Isn't that a father's duty?"

"Yes, Rufino, of course. But Brother Peter can do that. I have to accept what I am able to do, and I must look ahead. Those yet to join us will be helped more by any good example I might give than by multiplying laws and regulations that might not fit their circumstances. Now don't look so sad. I'm not dead yet and, you will see, I will have more time this way to be a brother to you all. Be happy for me and with me. Let's sing some songs to gladden our hearts. Where did you put the violin I asked you to borrow, Rufino?"

My heart skipped a beat or two knowing that I was going to disappoint Francis. But no sense avoiding the question.

"Francis," I said, "I didn't bring one. I was too ashamed to ask anyone for a violin, afraid people would wonder why we would want one except to be frivolous and to have parties. I was afraid of disedifying them."

"I guess you did the right thing, Rufino," he said. But I could see he was disappointed. "I would truly have relished some songs on the violin," he went on, "and it would have helped with the song I composed and want to teach you. But the Lord will gladden me with a violin some other time, perhaps.

"Anyhow, let me sing my song for you so you can learn it and then we can all sing it together." He closed his eyes and, making as though he were actually rubbing a bow across the strings of an imaginary violin he held, he began in a soft tenor voice:

Most high, all-powerful, all good, Lord!
All praise is yours, all glory, all honor
And all blessing.
To you, alone, Most High, do they belong.
No mortal lips are worthy
To pronounce your name.
All praise be yours, my Lord, through all that you have made,
And first my lord Brother Sun,
Who brings the day; and light you give to us through him.
How beautiful is he, how radiant in all his splendor!
Of you, Most High, he bears the likeness.
All praise be yours, my Lord, through Sister Moon and Stars;
In the heavens you have made them, bright
And precious and fair.
All praise be yours, my Lord, through Brothers Wind and Air,
And fair and stormy, all the weather's moods,
By which you cherish all that you have made.
All praise be yours, my Lord, through Sister Water,
So useful, lowly, precious and pure.
All praise be yours, my Lord, through Brother Fire,
Through whom you brighten up the night,
How beautiful is he, how joyous! Full of power

and strength.
All praise be yours, my Lord, through Sister Earth,
our Mother,
> *Who feeds us in her sovereignty and produces*
> *Various fruits with colored flowers and herbs.*

He put down his imaginary fiddle and, opening his eyes, said, "I think there is more to the song than that, but the Lord hasn't taught me the words yet."

"It's beautiful," said John. "Sing it again, a little at a time, so we can learn it. Leo, why don't you write down the words so we won't forget them?"

"A good idea," agreed Leo. "Wait till I find our pen and something to write on."

Far into the night we sat by the fire, singing Francis' song over and over till we had learned it. Brother Anthony, asking if it had a title and learning there was none, said that he thought Canticle of the Creatures would serve well, so Leo wrote that over the lyrics he had copied.

After awhile we just sat there in the warmth of the fire, each of us lost in his own thoughts and enjoying the peace and the brotherhood that the song had produced in us. Finally Francis stiffly stood up, said good night to us all, paused to adjust his vision to the darkness and went off to the chapel and cave in the clearing above. Then each of us followed him out to go to rest. A crescent moon hung above us amid the stars. The storm had passed.

I was restless. Sleep escaped me. Francis' news that

he would retire from governing the Brothers was too unsettling, provoked too many conjectures to allow sleep. Finally I gave up and went outside, careful not to awaken the others but confident that Brother John's heavy snoring would cover any noise I might make.

Sitting on a stone near the well, I settled down to listen to the night sounds and to think out again what Francis' announcement might mean for all of us. A nearby sound roused me and, turning my head, I looked squarely into the eyes of Bandit, who gave my face a quick lick with his generous tongue.

"Bandit," I whispered, wiping my face on my sleeve, "I appreciate your affection but don't be so stealthy. Give a fellow more warning."

He pricked up his ears, looking toward the upper chapel.

Then I heard it, too. A violin! Someone was playing a violin up there! Francis? But how did he get a violin? Whoever was playing it was a master. And what a beautiful melody! I had never heard the piece before— I would never have forgotten it.

Without being aware of it I was drawn up the path toward the clearing, the music like a net that had captured me and pulled me to its source. Bandit and I came to the clearing and stood under the acorn tree opposite the chapel door. On a pillar of stones not far from the chapel stood what must have been an angel. I didn't know, I had never seen one. But the figure seemed made of light which dazzled with an iridescence beyond my telling. I can only say that it was the most beautiful sight I had ever seen before and have ever seen since. Bandit made a sort of moan and wagged his tail.

The angel, if such it was, held a violin equally as luminous as itself and drew a bow across it to give a melody that was enough to take one's breath from his lungs, beyond all possible sounds this world could produce, so sweet and stirring the sound. I don't know how long I stood there, so caught up was I in the notes rising to a crescendo. But I knew that in another moment, out of pure ecstasy, my soul would shatter.

It was over. The final crystal notes seemed to rest on the stillness like diamonds on velvet. The brilliant light quickly faded and was gone. From inside the chapel I heard a muffled sob that made tears come to my own eyes. Quickly I seized Bandit by his collar and soundlessly we retreated from the clearing back to the well.

The good God had taught me again how much he loved Francis, that even such a small thing as gratifying his desire to hear a violin was not beyond his care. I felt a twinge of remorse within me as I recalled how lacking in trust I had been that God would care for the Order no matter how Francis' retirement was received by the Brothers. Why do I always take the unexpected with the grace of a cow on ice?

CHAPTER

5

NOT THE NEXT MORNING, as Francis had said, but three days later we were on our way to Assisi. He had decided that Brother Anthony would profit from a few more days of rest before continuing any journey. Brother John saw to it that Anthony ate well and had time to sleep.

Rising long before dawn on the fourth day, we had heard Mass, which Leo celebrated for us, prayed Matins and Lauds, had a bite to eat and then we started off for Assisi as the sun was lightening the sky beyond the mountains to the east.

Once again we walked in single file, down the path toward Sant' Urbano, some cuckoos welcoming the morning as it grew there in the east. John again led the way, picking out the safest route along the path that here and there had been washed away. Francis followed him, his hood over his head, to protect his eyes from too much light, and the rest of us following along behind. Each of us was deep in his own thought and prayer, but aware enough to return a few greetings from people taking the morning milk from the family cow in the fields outside the town.

Not entering the town, we passed by Sant' Urbano and continued on our way toward Terni. It was going to be a beautiful day and we were in no hurry, so I settled my spirit to enjoy the walk and to look for God along the way. Francis always reminded us that our brothers and sisters, creatures like ourselves, were able to point out to us that God had passed this way. Each swallow gathering its morning food for its young, each bee going from flower to flower, yes, every leaf and blade of grass had something to tell us about God, our Father. I always asked a flower or even a stone in the road three questions: What can you tell me, Sister Flower, about God? What can you tell me about yourself? And what can you tell me about me? These smaller creatures have such wisdom! And they share it willingly.

We had stopped twice to pray the Divine Office of Prime and Terce from the breviary that Leo carried in the pack on his back. By midday, when it was time for Sext and we were in the outskirts of Terni, Francis asked John to lead us off the road to some shade under a large oak tree. There, a cicada giving our psalms a musical accompaniment, we prayed the Office.

As we stretched out in the grass for a bit of rest under the tree, Leo brought out of his knapsack a half-loaf of bread and some cheese that we hadn't eaten at the hermitage, along with a gourd of water from the well. I wondered if it might turn out to be wine, another miracle like the one we witnessed a few nights ago. But as we passed the food around, giving thanks for God's providence, when the gourd came to me it was only water. Not that I complained!

We had hardly started to eat when we heard a little bell, and not far away. All of us knew at once that it was a leper's bell. And sure enough, around the bend in the road, not fifty feet from us, came a leper—a woman and not old, I think, although it would be hard to say with certainty, for the disease had already disfigured the poor soul's face so. She walked with difficulty because her legs were so swollen and covered with sores; burlap was wrapped around her puffy and infected feet.

I don't know about Brother Anthony, but the rest of us had all worked in leprosariums at one time or another, ministering to these poor brothers and sisters. Even so, the sight of lepers always gave me a jolt and I had to get used to being with them before I felt comfortable.

But not Francis. Jumping up and running to the leper as if to greet his dearest friend, he gave her such a hug that she almost toppled over. He invited her to join us under the tree for something to eat and helped her to hobble in our direction. We made room for our guest and Francis darted around gathering up some bread, some cheese, the gourd of water, to offer her.

Benedetta was her name, she said. "You truly are a blessed one," Francis said. Benedetta was busy trying to put food in her mouth as best she could, her fingers grotesquely swollen, cracked and bleeding, sores around her mouth. But Francis' statement about being a blessed person brought her to a sudden stop.

"Blessed?" she croaked. "Do you call this blessed?

Look at me. Take a good look if you can stand it. I once was beautiful, I once had thick and shiny black hair where you see these few wisps of gray now. My father had to beat off with a stick the young men of Terni who wanted to marry me. I would have had a handsome husband from a good family, I would have been a mother of beautiful children, I would have been so happy. And now look at me. Blessed am I? You're crazy. And cruel, too, to say such a thing."

"I know, Benedetta," Francis nodded. "Life does not look very hopeful when you don't feel well, especially when you carry a burden like yours. But you must believe that God can help you, that he wants to help you. Jesus, who cured so many sick, many of them lepers, can still cure. We do not have to go to Jerusalem to find him as we would have to do when he lived there. Now that he is risen from the dead, he is not confined to any one place nor to any time. He is with us now everywhere and anywhere. He is the curer of us all. Still. So don't lose hope, good Benedetta, and in the meantime let Jesus carry this cross of yours with you. He is an expert when it comes to crosses, and he will show you how it's done. Now, let's take a look at those hands of yours and your feet. We are skilled at caring for people with this illness that you have."

"Sir," she said (I'm sure she had no idea who Francis was), "if you can do anything to make my hands and feet better, I would be grateful."

Francis pulled out of his sleeve a handkerchief, a

piece of cloth, really, that he had been using to wipe his eyes which watered so often. "Angelo," he said, "hand me the gourd of water." He wet the cloth and started to dab Benedetta's hands, covered as they were with open sores, scabs and dried matter and blood. I could hardly bear to look at them. But Francis gently cleaned away the accumulation of dirt and matter while she looked on. She had no feeling in her hands, of course, so she didn't complain once of what would cause anyone else to scream and yell.

"Now your feet," Francis said, beginning to unwrap the burlap from around them. Her feet were as bad as her hands and far more dirty from the dust of the road and the lack of care she had given them. So he started to cleanse her feet, too, and from the looks of them I doubted we would have enough water or he a big enough rag.

"Hey!" Benedetta cried out. Startled, Francis jumped, thinking that he had somehow hurt her, I suppose.

"Look at my hands!" She held them out and the swelling was gone; they seemed to be healing right before our eyes. "And my feet! They're getting better!"

It was true. Like watching a butterfly emerge from its chrysalis, a beautiful-looking young woman was appearing from behind the sores and scabs of leprosy. She jumped up and began to examine herself closely, paying no attention to half a dozen gaping friars.

"Look at me, look at me," she yelled, her voice now strong and pleasant. "I'm cured! How did you do that? Who are you, anyway?" she asked, looking at Francis.

"Don't look at me," he said. "I'm surprised, too. I was asking Jesus to heal you as I cleaned your hands and feet, but I didn't know he was going to be so prompt about it. I thought you would get better slowly. But didn't I tell you that you had a special name? That you are blessed? You surely are!"

"Oh, sir, whatever your name is, God bless you!" She was crying and laughing at the same time. "Please, please don't think ill of me, but I have to go show my mother and father that I am healed." With that she grabbed Francis around the neck, gave him a kiss and, turning, ran up the road toward Terni.

We all just stood there. Miracles seemed to be a part of our life lately.

"Francis," I asked, "did you know that Jesus would heal her when you suggested cleaning her hands?"

"No, I didn't know. I hoped that the Lord would take pity on her and turn her heart to him, but I didn't know. We have to hope. And now we have to hope that the Lord's cure for Benedetta's leprosy will be a cure for her soul, too. She did not know me, nor should she; but she doesn't know the Lord either, and that is serious. I think that our hope will be gratified: She will come to love the Lord, she will become a good wife and mother."

We sat down again under the tree to finish our interrupted lunch. Brother Anthony, who had been watching all of this with even more wonder than the rest of us, said: "Father Francis, you seem to have a special love for lepers. Why is that?"

"That's true, Brother Anthony. Some day, when I can manage it, do you know what I would like to do?" Anthony shook his head. "I would like to minister to lepers again, as I did when the Lord first called me. And why? Because it seems to me that there I can best experience Jesus. I know that Jesus gives me in that most Blessed Sacrament of Communion his Body and his Blood as my food and drink. I believe that, although I see only bread and wine and taste only bread and wine.

"I know that Jesus speaks to me when I read or hear the Holy Scriptures. I believe that, although I hear a priest's voice. But when I care for a leper, touch a leper, feed or bathe a leper, I believe that I am caring for, touching, feeding and bathing the poor Jesus who took on our flesh.

"Saint Paul tells us that Jesus 'emptied himself' to do that. He set aside the glory of heaven, set aside his divinity as best he could, to become a human being. We think that it is such a grandiose thing to be a human being, don't we? We put gems on our fingers, dress ourselves in silk and brocade, put a crown on our heads and we strut around. And it's true that we are marvelous bits of creation.

"But as fine a piece of work as we are, God had to strip himself to nothing to get down to our level. If you can imagine filling a burlap sack with precious stones, gold and crowns, that immeasurable treasure is divinity. Now empty out the treasure and what have you left? The burlap bag. That's what we are, and that's what Jesus took on, setting aside his wealth.

"Truly, there is not a great deal of difference between the sleek and healthy king with a crown on his head, and the leper covered with sores begging at the side of the road. The differences are superficial.

"It is the leper, though, that makes me realize what Jesus did in assuming our flesh. His love for us is so immense, so tender, that he took on the flesh of the leper. He desires so much to be one of us that he takes on the sores, the utter poverty, of the scorned and feared leper.

"Yes, it is in poverty, in sickness and rejection that we experience who we really are as human beings, and we discover the overpowering love of God for us.

"Poverty is a secret, Brother Anthony, and there are few indeed who know it. Even among ourselves. It is the key to understanding Christmas, Easter and the whole life of Jesus in between. And our life, too. Now let's give thanks to God for this food we have shared and ask his blessing on us as we continue our journey to Assisi and on our sister Benedetta as she picks up her life again."

We spent a few moments praying to God, thanking him for his marvelous ways. We helped Leo pack up what was left and started off again along the road that led into the countryside. We came to a rise and there it lay below us, a patchwork of crops, fields and vineyards soaking up the warm sunshine. Here and there a pond glistened. A valley of contentment and peace.

Far up the valley to the north lay Assisi, my home. And there, too, many, many friars were wondering where Francis was. They were wondering what would become of the Order in the days to come. Not to worry, I thought, as we started down into the valley, for the Lord, the Lord who brings peace, is with us.

EPILOGUE

ONLY LAST WEEK BROTHER LEO came here to the Carceri where I am staying during the summer months, up here on the mountain above Assisi. He brought news of a request by Brother Bonaventure, the new Minister General of the Order. It seems that Brother Bonaventure wants to write an official biography of Francis to separate facts from the legends and fables that one hears about him. Leo knew of the pages I had written some years ago about our days spent in the Rieti Valley after Francis' return from the Holy Places, the days that led to his retirement from the leadership of the Brothers. He said I must send my writings to Brother Bonaventure, for they will be important, coming from someone who knew Francis so well. But before I send them off, it is only right that I bring to a close, in a few words, the end part of Francis' life as I saw it.

That day that we strode off from Terni toward Assisi where so many friars were gathered and awaited Francis' return, I was at peace with Francis' decision to give over leadership of the Order to Brother Peter Catanii. I trusted Francis' desire to lead us now by example rather than by legislation. I trusted God's protection and direction of this movement he had brought about under Francis.

But of course none of us—not Francis, not Peter, not I—had any inkling of what lay ahead. Francis did hand over the reins of leadership to Brother Peter. For almost all the friars it was a sad moment, for we all loved and admired him so. He was not only our brother, he was our father as well. But it was evident that he could barely see and had to be guided about and cared for. Too, his health was frail from dropsy and consumption. The burden of overseeing the fraternity was patently too much for him. So, as I say, it was with sadness, but with our acceptance, that Francis stepped aside and Peter Catanii became our Minister General.

And then Peter, strong and energetic Peter, took sick and quickly died only a few months after taking office. He lies buried under the south wall of Our Lady of the Angels, the little church where he had joined Francis in the early days of the Order. His fame as a holy friar began to attract pilgrims to his grave, so Francis, lest miracles by Peter's intercession detract from the special pardon (known as the Portiuncula Indulgence) that the pope had granted to that place, commanded Peter to work no wonders. And Peter, obedient in death as in life, had complied.

Francis then chose Brother Elias to succeed Peter. It was a choice that disappointed many of us, and our fears later proved correct, but I must admit that Elias loved Francis and did all he could to care for Francis and carry out his wishes for as long as he lived.

Being free now of the governance of the Brothers, Francis gave himself even more intently to being an example for us of what a true friar should be. Despite his poor health, he continued with his fasts and vigils and, as best he could, with his forays to preach in the towns and villages of central Italy.

Even when the Lord stamped into Francis' body his own wounds received upon the cross, making him even physically more like the suffering Jesus he so loved, Francis continued to go out to preach. About these wounds in his hands, feet and side, something should be said, for the news of that great favor has spread among the people. However, since this is an account of what I actually witnessed, I will leave to Leo the relating of that event there on Mount Alverna, for he was present. All I can say of it is that he truly had these wounds, for I helped care for Francis during the days before his death.

Francis had become very weak. The fasting he insisted on continuing, his illnesses and now the pain and loss of blood that went with the wounds that Jesus had pressed on him, all these brought Francis close to death. Sister Clare had asked that a hut be built at San Damiano so that she and her Sisters might care for him. During the day Francis would remain in the hut because his eyes, although now sightless, were tormented by the bright sun. Only at dusk and before sunrise would he venture out to enjoy the aromas of flowers and mown grass, the sound of his friends the birds singing their morning praises or evening song.

The days were often spent in torment from the heat and from pain. At times mice would scurry about the hut, sometimes startling him as they ran across his face.

He was most careful lest anyone see his wounds. But helping to care for him, providing his needs, I saw on several occasions the blood-soaked rags he had used to wrap around his hands and feet. And on one occasion, moved by inquisitiveness, I confess, I suggested that he remove his habit that I might clean it. Helping take it off, I placed my hand on his side, touching an open wound. My hand came away with blood on my fingers. Francis cried out, wincing with the pain, and looked reprovingly at me.

"God forgive you, Rufino," he said, and I was ashamed.

So I can attest that Francis did have wounds in his feet and hands and side. The man I knew who was in his spirit a perfect model of Christ was also externally conformed to his likeness.

These wounds, of course, added to his suffering and continuing decline in health. But it was precisely during those waning days that he added another stanza to the song he had composed in praise of the creatures. He had previously added a stanza and had it sung to the bishop and the mayor of Assisi who were at odds. And, believe it or not, the song was a vehicle of grace, touching both their hearts and bringing them to reconcile their differences.

*All praise be yours, my Lord, through those who
grant pardon*
for love of you; through those who endure
Sickness and trial.
Happy those who endure in peace,
By you, Most High, they will be crowned.

The final stanza sang of Sister Death, who had become
more and more a constant companion, waiting to
accompany Francis' soul to heaven. If you have not yet
heard the words, I include them in this testimony.

All praise be yours, my Lord, through Sister Death,
From whose embrace no mortal can escape.
Woe to those who die in mortal sin!
Happy those She finds doing your will!
The second death can do no harm to them.
Praise and bless my Lord and give him thanks,
And serve him with great humility.

The rest of the story I am sure everyone knows: that on
the evening of October 3, 1226, at St. Mary of the
Angels, Francis' soul went to meet the Lord he had
loved and served so well; that we took his body to the
church of St. George in Assisi where he had learned his
ABC's as a boy, stopping by San Damiano so that Sister
Clare and the other Sisters might say farewell to their
Father. Now, of course, he is buried under the altar in
the lower church of the huge monument planned and
built by Brother Elias.

But don't think that these words spell out the end

of the story of Francis. He, who loved to hear the epic tale of the Chanson de Roland and of King Arthur and the knights of the Round Table, now is the topic of many tales and legends that tell of noble deeds and pure hearts. Francis still challenges hearts the world around to serve the Great King, the Lord Jesus, with similar fervor and abandon.